THIS IS ME! 2022

REACH FOR THE STARS

Edited By Byron Tobolik

First published in Great Britain in 2022 by:

Young Writers
Remus House
Coltsfoot Drive
Peterborough
PE2 9BF
Telephone: 01733 890066
Website: www.youngwriters.co.uk

All Rights Reserved
Book Design by Ashley Janson
© Copyright Contributors 2022
Softback ISBN 978-1-80015-981-5

Printed and bound in the UK by BookPrintingUK
Website: www.bookprintinguk.com
YB0504W

FOREWORD

For Young Writers' latest competition This Is Me, we asked primary school pupils to look inside themselves, to think about what makes them unique, and then write a poem about it! They rose to the challenge magnificently and the result is this fantastic collection of poems in a variety of poetic styles.

Here at Young Writers our aim is to encourage creativity in children and to inspire a love of the written word, so it's great to get such an amazing response, with some absolutely fantastic poems. It's important for children to focus on and celebrate themselves and this competition allowed them to write freely and honestly, celebrating what makes them great, expressing their hopes and fears, or simply writing about their favourite things. This Is Me gave them the power of words. The result is a collection of inspirational and moving poems that also showcase their creativity and writing ability.

I'd like to congratulate all the young poets in this anthology, I hope this inspires them to continue with their creative writing.

CONTENTS

Blessed Robert Widmerpool Catholic Voluntary Academy, Clifton

Nathaniel Pilat (9)	1
Maia Browitt (10)	2
Lily Dufaj (9)	3
Dwayne Monge (9)	4
Leo Mahon-Young (9)	5
Kian Harvey (9)	6
Archie Joel Wallace (9)	7
Freya Leek (10)	8
Alexander Bucior (10)	9
Chace Corpe (10)	10
Maci Fowlds (10)	11
Kai Greatorex (10)	12
Rio Greatorex (10)	13
Marcel Kacak (9)	14
Sophia Smith (9)	15
Hayley Edanee Cantos (10)	16
Oskar Turner (10)	17
Alex Byrne (9)	18

Edwards Primary School, Castlederg

Jessica McCreery (11)	19
Brooklyn Williamson (11)	20
Emily Crilly (11)	21
Lily Clarke (11)	22
Luke Doherty (10)	23
Alison Williamson (11)	24
Shannon Smyth (11)	25
Carter McCreery (11)	26
Callum Kee (10)	27
Jamie Rogers (11)	28

Gayhurst School, Gerrards Cross

Charlotte Gordon (6)	29
Ezra Rashti (7)	30
Jayin Shah (6)	31
Pippa Othen (6)	32
Sianna Braich (6)	33
Enid Willcox (7)	34
Ishaan Patel (7)	35
Charles Daniel (7)	36
Sophie Houghton (6)	37
Bella Van Nieuwenhuijzen (6)	38
Michael (7)	39
Benjamin Arch (7)	40
Emily Harrington (6)	41
Arran Jolly (6)	42
Thomas Baker (7)	43
Lottie Houghton (6)	44
Arjan Saigal (7)	45
Xander Ashelford (7)	46
Thomas Singleton (7)	47
Freya Moscovitch (6)	48
Freddie Ford (7)	49
Isabel Brodie (7)	50
Kavish Hajare (6)	51
Mahi Patel (6)	52
Summer Geromoschos (7)	53
Sarah Walsh (6)	54
Florie Misan (6)	55
Suhavi Kaur (6)	56
Chloe Dingley (7)	57
Alana Peppitt (6)	58
Calum Ives (7)	59
Sebastian Gordon (6)	60
Arthur Bettridge (7)	61

Kilmartin Primary School, Kilmartin

Felix Malcolm (10)	62
Belle Rusden (10)	63
Calleigh McNair (9)	64
Sophie Kerr (10)	65

Regents Park Community Primary School, Small Heath

Ummayyah Shakil (8)	66
Inaaya Khan (9)	67
Ayaan Ul Gani (7)	68
Maria Hussain (10)	69
Seema Al-Shamery (10)	70
Abid Hossain (7)	71
Reyel Kazi (10)	72
Zakariya Mahmood (7)	73
Rahaf Albarkoly (10)	74
Sanjida Islam (8)	75
Anas Sultan (7)	76
Mustapha Bigira (8)	77
Maesha Rahman (10)	78
Aatikah Begum (10)	79
Fozya Jemal	80
Siddig Mostafa (11)	81
Inayah Mehran (8)	82
Umaymah Uddin (8)	83
Mahad Miah (9)	84
Hasanah Sadhiq (10)	85
Samiha Uddin (7)	86
Manaal Shaiban (11)	87
Amina Arshad (8)	88
Sumaiyya Hussain (8)	89
Noor-Zainab Ali (8)	90
Iqra Hussain (7)	91
Muntaha Uddin (9)	92
Hawwa Afzal (7)	93

St Peter's Brafferton CEVA Primary School, Helperby

Finley Abbott (10)	94
Ruby Gaunt (9)	95
Zander van Leijen (10)	96
Emily Dwyer (10)	97
Olivia Sherwood (11)	98
Henry Hambling (8)	99
Poppy Gaunt	100
Josie Wise (8)	101
Mia Norman (10)	102
Sebastian Medi-Sherwood (8)	103
Louisa Chadwick (10)	104

The Gateway Primary Academy, Dartford

Sophie Harman (9)	105
Janna Oyedeji (9)	106
Eliza Huhulski (9)	107
Fairmah Asare (9)	108
Faith Francois (9)	109
Isla Coogan (8)	110
Scarlett Eve Leachman (10)	111
Andrew George Gray (10)	112

The Thomas Coram CE School, Berkhamsted

Ava Hillier (9)	113
Kenny Vile (9)	114
Holly Ormondroyd (9)	115
Ava Lambley-Webb (10)	116
Sophie Carlton (10)	117
Elliot Goodison (10)	118
Billy Kirk (10)	119
Ella Hillier (9)	120
Max Culwick (10)	121
James Bedlow (10)	122
Lucy Bedlow (7)	123
Sofia Fornelli Gajos (7)	124
Heidi Moffatt (8)	125
Charlotte Goodison (8)	126

Poppy Warr (10)	127
James Pierce (10)	128
Austin Jenkin-Seymour (10)	129
Oscar Nowaczyk (9)	130
Lola Rowe-Waller (7)	131
Evie Hardy	132
Rosa Drath (8)	133
Eliza Lines (7)	134
Grace Howard (9)	135
Joseph Kelly (7)	136
Ozzie Page (9)	137
Evie Curtis (10)	138
Freddie Bannister (9)	139
Henry Winnett (9)	140
Noah Cummins (7)	141
Thomas Crane (10)	142
Zach Rae (9)	143
Ivy Thurley (8)	144
Sky Seaton (7)	145
Josh George (9)	146
Mabel Thomas (7)	147
Alex Newman (8)	148
Wilfred Foxwell-Moss (7)	149
Effie Weedon-Grant (7)	150
Jarvis Madoc Poulton (9)	151
Chester Dawson (7)	152
Gregory Cummins (10)	153
Harvey Skerm (8)	154
Sam Gold (7)	155
Sammy Branch (9)	156
Nina Teixeira (8)	157
Eleanor Badham (9)	158
Kenzi Bonnell (8)	159
Winston Collett (8)	160
Charlotte Nelson (10)	161
Martin-Cooley (10)	162
Isabella Keane (8)	163
Dexter Barfoot (8)	164
Luke Jenkins (10)	165
Avaley Marley (8)	166
Amelia Rae (7)	167
Samuel Edwards (7)	168
Barnaby Owen (8)	169

Tommy Hobley (10)	170
Ryan John (8)	171
Freya Harrison (8)	172
Hannah Manns (8)	173
Lorelei Stanford (8)	174
Raffy Chemin-Walker	175
Flora Harrison (7)	176
Darcy Prince (8)	177
Eliza Prince (8)	178
James Dowling (7)	179
Emily Ainsworth (8)	180
Imogen Freeman (8)	181
Will Goodman (8)	182

Thornton Primary School, Thornton-Cleveleys

Jayden Hislop (9)	183
River Garside (11)	184
Kitty Woffenden (10)	186
Charleigh-Jo Taylor-Stansfield (10)	187
Leah Wilson (9)	188
Timur Whiteside (10)	189
Evie Jones (10)	190
Courtney Leigh Flackett (11)	191
Krystian Jegier (9)	192
Ava Taylor (8)	193
Emelia Rae (8)	194
Ruby Hill (7)	195
Samuel Mays (8)	196
Sophie Reidy (7)	197
Mason Twiss (10)	198
Ellie Turner (9)	199
Callum McCluskey (9)	200
Mae Badenoch (7)	201
Lewis Chantler (7)	202
Violet Anderson (10)	203
Phoebe Moore-Rainford (10)	204
Brooke Bamforth (8)	205
Thomas Grant (7)	206
Daniel Grant (7)	207
Freddie Thompson (7)	208

THE POEMS

It's About Me

I am a little boy who's always longing for a cuddle from my mum,
As the days go by, I realise I need to grow,
I learnt how to shower by myself,
I want to be independent like a grown man,
But I am still a little boy,
Always longing to play with my friends,
Laughing and talking nonsense like a little boy,
I love to say hello to cheer up other people around me,
Even though they are strangers to me,
Because we are all human and created by our almighty God,
I am still a little boy, happy and innocent,
I am proud of what I am doing today,
This is me, always stay happy,
Spread happiness and respect other humans.

Nathaniel Pilat (9)
Blessed Robert Widmerpool Catholic Voluntary Academy, Clifton

Maia Browitt

I'm Maia Browitt, I'm normally very happy,
Sometimes I get angry and it makes me
very snappy.
I am ten years and 30 days old,
The one thing I hate the most is being cold.
The person I admire the most is my
wonderful mum,
Even though sometimes she can be a pain
in the bum.
I have a hamster called Daisy,
But most of the time, she is very lazy.
When I grow older, I would like to be a vet,
Animals are the kindest creatures I've ever met.
Thank you for reading this poem about me,
I hope it makes you full of glee.

Maia Browitt (10)
Blessed Robert Widmerpool Catholic Voluntary Academy, Clifton

This Is Me

Lily Dufaj is my name,
Clifton is the place where I live,
I am as colourful as a rainbow,
I am as cute as a lollipop,
I am as small as a gnome,
Purple is the colour I choose!
White chocolate takes away my blues,
I dream of going to the moon and back,
Noodles are my favourite food!
And boba is always good!
I really want to study in college,
I wish I had a little sister,
But I'm lucky I have a little brother,
I like to play with my friends and have fun.

Lily Dufaj (9)
Blessed Robert Widmerpool Catholic Voluntary Academy, Clifton

Grass

There are such things as the tall, green lines,
In fields, in forests, and even vines,
In your front and back garden, and your playground,
In many areas, grass is around.
It blows in your garden and in the wild,
Wish! Woosh! Don't worry, it is very mild.
It's like a small, green tree everywhere in sight;
A line that sees if you're sad or in a fight,
There are such things as the tall, green lines,
In fields, in forests, and even vines.

Dwayne Monge (9)
Blessed Robert Widmerpool Catholic Voluntary Academy, Clifton

Cats

Adorable, agile, affectionate,
the fluff balls make me smile.
While they are in a pile,
sitting on my lap,
taking a nap.

They are always my friend.
That I can depend on to be,
the little love I need.

And when it's time to leave,
I believe we achieved our goal.
To see it to the end
and to be relieved.

They will always be, a part of me.

Leo Mahon-Young (9)
Blessed Robert Widmerpool Catholic Voluntary Academy, Clifton

Type One Diabetes

My type one diabetes is like a curse,
But I suppose things could be a lot worse.
My life is measured by a high or a low,
Going up and down like a yo-yo.
Carb counting, tech and insulin,
Some days are perfect which is a win.
My Dexcom keeps me on track,
My type one can't hold me back.
This condition I will continue to endure,
Until the day we have a cure.

Kian Harvey (9)
Blessed Robert Widmerpool Catholic Voluntary Academy, Clifton

This Is Archie!

- **A** lways happy like the sun shining on a summer's day
- **R** aring and ready to go
- **C** aring, cheerful, curious, calm, cheeky, cool as ice
- **H** as a heart of gold that's as big as the universe
- **I** ndependent, inquisitive, imaginative, inspiring
- **E** nergetic like a cheetah running across the wild, open plain.

Archie Joel Wallace (9)
Blessed Robert Widmerpool Catholic Voluntary Academy, Clifton

Freya

Hi, I am Freya, this is me,
I love dancing and competing to win trophies,
Swimming in the sea makes me want to splash,
With fun and laughter as the waves around me crash,
This isn't my only happy time, as my best friend, she's the kindest,
Makes me feel warm inside when she shares her Winders.

Freya Leek (10)
Blessed Robert Widmerpool Catholic Voluntary Academy, Clifton

My Two Dogs

They are two white dogs,
Both fluffy and cuddly,
They both like to fetch the ball,
They want to take them all.
Both white with brown spots,
They eat lots and lots,
They're lazy at night,
And crazy in the day,
Always there to play with you,
As long as you have a ball.

Alexander Bucior (10)
Blessed Robert Widmerpool Catholic Voluntary Academy, Clifton

My Favourite

My name is Chace,
I can kick a football up to space.
My favourite subject is math,
I have been told I am a bit daft.
My favourite colour is green,
And I don't like people who are mean.
My favourite season is summer,
Winter can be a real bummer.

Chace Corpe (10)
Blessed Robert Widmerpool Catholic Voluntary Academy, Clifton

Mum

You love me,
Without reason,
You show me,
That you care.

You take me through,
Each season,
You're always kind,
And fair.

My life with you,
Is never humdrum,
There are no conditions,
With love from you, my mum.

Maci Fowlds (10)
Blessed Robert Widmerpool Catholic Voluntary Academy, Clifton

About Me

K ind-hearted
A uthentic
I maginative

G enerous
R eliable
E ager
A mbitious
T alented
O ptimistic
R elatable
E nergetic
X factor.

Kai Greatorex (10)
Blessed Robert Widmerpool Catholic Voluntary Academy, Clifton

The Poem About Rio

R apid
I ntelligent
O pen-hearted

G reat
R easonable
E xcellent
A mbitious
T alented
O riginal
R eliable
E nergetic
X factor.

Rio Greatorex (10)
Blessed Robert Widmerpool Catholic Voluntary Academy, Clifton

Cute Animal

J olts like a cheetah
E levating on top of the hot sand
R eal as can be
B obbing up and down like a boat
O bserve the cuteness of this creature
A bsolutely incredible species this is.

Marcel Kacak (9)
Blessed Robert Widmerpool Catholic Voluntary Academy, Clifton

Friends

F orever together
R emember to be loyal
I will always be by your side
E very step you take, I take too
N ever be apart
D o everything as sisters
S till be yourself.

Sophia Smith (9)
Blessed Robert Widmerpool Catholic Voluntary Academy, Clifton

My Best Friend

I have a best friend,
Tall and magnificent,
She always inspires me,
To be someone different.

I care for her so much,
And she does too,
So I wrote this to tell her,
I care about you.

Hayley Edanee Cantos (10)
Blessed Robert Widmerpool Catholic Voluntary Academy, Clifton

I Would Hog A Dog

I would hog a dog,
One day, on my morning jog,
I saw a dog,
The dog was lost in the fog,
Hidden under a log,
I named the dog Zog,
And hogged the dog,
I still would hog a dog.

Oskar Turner (10)
Blessed Robert Widmerpool Catholic Voluntary Academy, Clifton

All About Alex

I am a boy,
Alex is my name,
And I really like,
Roblox video games.
Although, pizza is my thing,
It gives me a zing,
That great round ring,
To me is the biggest thing!

Alex Byrne (9)
Blessed Robert Widmerpool Catholic Voluntary Academy, Clifton

How To Make Me

You will need:
5lbs of kindness,
10lbs of doughnuts,
3lbs of loving sunsets and sunrises,
20lbs of loving dogs, especially mine,
4 teaspoons of liking to read,
6lbs of being a good helper.

Now you need to:
Mix kindness, being a good helper and arts and crafts in a bowl.
Then in a different bowl, mix doughnuts, sunsets, sunrises and liking to read.
After, mix both mixtures together and add a dash of loving dogs, especially mine!
Put in the oven and...
Voila!

Jessica McCreery (11)
Edwards Primary School, Castlederg

This Is Me!

This is me, I like to play,
I play with my brother all day.

I like to play on my Xbox,
On the weekends, I wear fluffy socks.

I like to sleep in my bed,
Or maybe watch TV instead.

On Fridays, we play Cluedo,
But sometimes we play Uno.

My favourite hero is Spider-Man,
Because he can lend a helping hand.

This is me, ready to move school,
But I think it'll be cool.

Brooklyn Williamson (11)
Edwards Primary School, Castlederg

This Is Emily!

T iny in height
H air is long
I have lots of friends
S maller than my friend

I love school
S mile with happiness

E ven nicer than a whale
M akes a great friend
I love my dogs
L ove my family and friends
Y ou are all so kind.

Emily Crilly (11)
Edwards Primary School, Castlederg

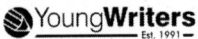

This Is Me!

L ittle in size
I like to dance
L iving in a house
Y ear 7 in school

C an do every subject in school
L oving
A rtistic
R eally helpful
K ind inside and out
E ncouraging.

Lily Clarke (11)
Edwards Primary School, Castlederg

Who Am I?

I have ginger hair.
I have blue eyes.
I love computers.
My favourite food is pizza.
I love playing on the iPad.
I love dogs.
I am a happy person.
Who am I?

Answer: *This is me, I am Luke.*

Luke Doherty (10)
Edwards Primary School, Castlederg

My Favourite Animal

I have sharp teeth.
I live in the sea.
If you see me, you will flee!
My favourite food is a seal.
If I am hungry enough, maybe you will be my next meal.
What am I?

Answer: A shark.

Alison Williamson (11)
Edwards Primary School, Castlederg

This Is Me
A kennings poem

I am a...
Horse rider,
Early riser,
Hockey player,
Morning runner,
Clear speaker,
Carrot eater,
Football player,
Midday swimmer,
Late-night muncher,
Sleep talker.

Shannon Smyth (11)
Edwards Primary School, Castlederg

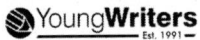

My Pizza Poem

P izza is my favourite food
I nside Domino's, I am happy
Z ebras don't like pizza
Z ombies like their pizza with brains
A nd I like mine with pepperoni.

Carter McCreery (11)
Edwards Primary School, Castlederg

My Favourite Sport

I'm round like the sun.
I'm like a spotty dog.
I get kicked a lot.
I spin in the air like a Frisbee.
Goallllll!
What am I?

Answer: A football.

Callum Kee (10)
Edwards Primary School, Castlederg

My Favourite Animal

I'm sometimes at the zoo.
I run pretty fast.
I have a medium-sized neck.
I might bite your fingers off sometimes.
What am I?

Answer: An ostrich.

Jamie Rogers (11)
Edwards Primary School, Castlederg

Charlotte

C at lover is me
H appy with my brother
A nimals are the best, especially my cats
R ome is my favourite capital city
L ottie is my short name
O ne of my favourite series of books is Magic Kittens
T homas is my best friend
T his is my name - Charlotte
E very animal is cute.

Charlotte Gordon (6)
Gayhurst School, Gerrards Cross

Ezra Rashti

My favourite football team is England,
I am a Portugal lover,
My favourite video game is FIFA 22,
My dream is to live in Brazil,
My favourite place is Manchester,
I am a Man United fan,
My favourite foods are mac and cheese,
Sushi, katsu curry and dumplings.
This is me.

Ezra Rashti (7)
Gayhurst School, Gerrards Cross

This Is Me

I am super sporty,
I am a great goalkeeper,
I am kind and helpful,
I am caring and selfless,
I am a chocolate eater,
I love laughter,
I support Liverpool,
I am an animal lover,
I love the beach when it is windy,
I love reading,
Do you?
This is me.

Jayin Shah (6)
Gayhurst School, Gerrards Cross

This Is Me

P arty planning
I am an adventurer
P erfect picture drawer
P eople painter
A mazing artist

O cean full of emotions
T eam player
H eroic hero
E xcited dancer
N ervous singer, that's me.

Pippa Othen (6)
Gayhurst School, Gerrards Cross

Sianna

S loths are sleepy and slow
I like to ride horses because they're cool
A nimals are cute with their fluffy coats
N aughty monkeys swinging through the trees
N attering and chattering as loud as can be
A dders! Do they like sums? I do!

Sianna Braich (6)
Gayhurst School, Gerrards Cross

This Is Me
A kennings poem

I am a...
Doughnut eater
Animal lover
Winter wisher
Hot chocolate slurper
An awesome helper
Great lady
Good singer
Helpful friend
Funny girl
Story teller
Flower lover
Bucket filler
My favourite colour is violet.

Enid Willcox (7)
Gayhurst School, Gerrards Cross

Ishaan Patel

A kennings poem

I am a...
Football striker,
Nintendo player,
Maths superstar,
Lego builder,
Pasta eater,
Brownie baker,
Arsenal fan,
Star Wars general,
Comic reader,
Funny joker.
My dream is to...
Play for Arsenal.

Ishaan Patel (7)
Gayhurst School, Gerrards Cross

Charles

C hocolate is yummy
H olidays are fun
A nimals are amazing
R unning is tiring
L unch is delicious
E very day of winter is cold
S uper Charlie.

This is me!

Charles Daniel (7)
Gayhurst School, Gerrards Cross

I Love Myself

S pring is my favourite month
O reo is my favourite dog toy
P enguins are my favourite animal
H olidays are fun
I n the night, Mummy reads us a bedtime story
E aster is amazing!

Sophie Houghton (6)
Gayhurst School, Gerrards Cross

This Is Me
A kennings poem

I am...
A bucket filler,
A rose lover,
A fruit eater,
As lovely as sunshine,
A thoughtful friend,
A curious girl,
A kind person,
An awesome reader,
A funny sister,
And a fantastic cook.

Bella Van Nieuwenhuijzen (6)
Gayhurst School, Gerrards Cross

This Is Me!

M y name is Michael
I like chips
C hords, I practise on my piano
H arry is my buddy
A ugust is my birthday
E aster is amazing
L eopards are my favourite

Michael (7)
Gayhurst School, Gerrards Cross

Me

A kennings poem

I am...
A chocolate eater,
A kind person,
A summer wisher,
A swimming lover,
A maths mastermind,
A great gamer,
A Lego builder,
A good reader,
A football player...
Are you?

Benjamin Arch (7)
Gayhurst School, Gerrards Cross

My Favourite Thing

I like to ride them.
They are cute.
When you ride them, you need to wear a helmet.
They like to eat hay.
They need to wear a saddle.
I love them.
What are they?

Answer: Horses.

Emily Harrington (6)
Gayhurst School, Gerrards Cross

All About Me!

A pples are amazing
R ainforests are incredible
R unning on the grass is fun
A flying peregrine falcon is my favourite animal
N ice is a good thing I try to be!

Arran Jolly (6)
Gayhurst School, Gerrards Cross

The Things I Love

J ogging is fun
O reos are so tasty
S teaks are yummy
E ating is fun
P laying with my friends makes me happy
H appy is the emotion that describes me!

Thomas Baker (7)
Gayhurst School, Gerrards Cross

Lottie

L ike horses
O ver fences
T rotting around the fields
T he bit between their teeth
I nto the distance, they gallop
E ventually coming to a halt.

Lottie Houghton (6)
Gayhurst School, Gerrards Cross

This Is Me
A kennings poem

I am a...
Nintendo player,
Good goalkeeper,
Chocolate eater,
Great gamer,
Cake baker,
Tottenham fan,
My dream is...
To be a football player.

This is me.

Arjan Saigal (7)
Gayhurst School, Gerrards Cross

My Name Is Xander

X -ray fish are amazing
A nimals make me happy
N o dinosaur can fly
D inosaurs are awesome
E lephants are slow
R ainforests are incredible.

Xander Ashelford (7)
Gayhurst School, Gerrards Cross

Thomas

T om is my friend
H appiness is my default emotion
O reos are tasty
M inecraft is the best
A nimals are amazing
S uper Thomas - this is me!

Thomas Singleton (7)
Gayhurst School, Gerrards Cross

Melodies

M elodies are in my head
U sing instruments is fun
S inging makes me happy
I magination is crazy
C ymbals are loud and noisy.

This is me!

Freya Moscovitch (6)
Gayhurst School, Gerrards Cross

My Favourite Thing

It is a big black box,
It does one thing, *whizz!*
It is in most people's houses.
I can't live without it.
I watch it.
What is it?

Answer: A TV.

Freddie Ford (7)
Gayhurst School, Gerrards Cross

My Amazing Riddle

I love them.
For my birthday, I would like one.
Mine would be called Daisy.
Dogs can run for a longer amount of time.
But I love...

Answer: Cats.

Isabel Brodie (7)
Gayhurst School, Gerrards Cross

Poem.Com

My favourite thing is a TV show,
I watch it all the time,
It has animals out of this world,
They only go forwards and back in a line,
And it begins with a P.

Kavish Hajare (6)
Gayhurst School, Gerrards Cross

Mahi

M agnificent - this is me!
A mazing - this is me!
H appiness is the emotion I normally feel
I ce cream is one of my favourite treats.

Mahi Patel (6)
Gayhurst School, Gerrards Cross

My Dream

My dream is to be a singer,
But I'll never be a swimmer.
So remember your dreams,
And never forget them,
Otherwise, you might be a threat to them.

Summer Geromoschos (7)
Gayhurst School, Gerrards Cross

Me

I love...
Cartwheels,
Headstands,
Shoulderstands,
Handstands,
YouTube,
TV,
Sparkles.
My dream is...
To have a pet unicorn.

Sarah Walsh (6)
Gayhurst School, Gerrards Cross

My Life

I love my mummy,
I love my bunnies,
I love pop and rock,
I love taking naps,
I love Australia,
I like dogs on my lap,
I love my life!

Florie Misan (6)
Gayhurst School, Gerrards Cross

What Is My Favourite Food?

It swims in the ocean.
You can eat it.
It is quite small.
I love it with chips and peas!
What is my favourite food?

Answer: Cod.

Suhavi Kaur (6)
Gayhurst School, Gerrards Cross

Happy Feelings

C hristmas is fun!
H appy is a good feeling
L oving sister - this is me!
O ctopi are funny
E ating is yummy.

Chloe Dingley (7)
Gayhurst School, Gerrards Cross

This Is Me!
A kennings poem

I am a...
Funny joker,
Llama lover,
Cake maker,
Playground player,
Story teller,
Cuddle monster!
What are you?

Alana Peppitt (6)
Gayhurst School, Gerrards Cross

Hoverboards

They are my favourite thing,
They are very fast,
Please wear a helmet,
They are very loud,
And they are quick too.

Calum Ives (7)
Gayhurst School, Gerrards Cross

Me!
A kennings poem

I am a...
Football star,
History explorer,
Wycombe fan,
Pizza lover,
And a funny, friendly boy.

Sebastian Gordon (6)
Gayhurst School, Gerrards Cross

I Am A...
A kennings poem

Dog lover,
Sporty person,
Chocolate eater,
Pokémon trader,
Kind person,
Biscuit eater.

Arthur Bettridge (7)
Gayhurst School, Gerrards Cross

Playground Loneliness

P ainfully waiting
L ast hour wasted
A ggravatingly boring
Y oung life wearing off
G rey clouds fill the sky
R olling a stone around my hands
O n my own again
U nder the weather
N ever cheering up
D own in the dumps

L ots of time wasted
O range skies fading away
N ever wanting to join in
E very other child playing
L et me tell you about me
I diot but misunderstood
N ice but naughty
E verything about me has an opposite
S nood over my face
S orrow.

Felix Malcolm (10)
Kilmartin Primary School, Kilmartin

What Makes Me, Me!

W hat makes me, me, well...
H ave you ever heard of my many passions?
A thletics and
T ennis, football and art

M eerkats I love, not as much as chickens
A nimals are a part of me
K angaroos and foxes
E els and dolphins
S ome are fluffy, some are slimy, but I love them all... I'm

M essy, not clean
E xcited, not calm

M y body is mine, my thoughts are mine
E verything about me makes me.

Belle Rusden (10)
Kilmartin Primary School, Kilmartin

What Makes Me

W illing to do things
H as way too much energy
A dores animals
T hinks too much

M y hobbies are gymnastics and drawing
A nd especially adores lambs
K eeps old photos
E nergetic
S ings

M akes lots of crafts
E ats mostly healthy things.

Calleigh McNair (9)
Kilmartin Primary School, Kilmartin

Myself

M y cat is as friendly as an upside-down umbrella!
Y ou don't know how kind I can be
S .O.L.E. learning is the best!
E ven if I'm sad, my dogs are as bouncy as frogs!
L iving things can be amazing
F or my cat, I would do anything!

Sophie Kerr (10)
Kilmartin Primary School, Kilmartin

All About Me

I am writing a poem all about me.
I love writing all about me,
And I love drawing all about me.
I love hearing all about me.
I am humming all about me.
I always hear my teacher giving my work
a 'well done'.
I love my life, it's all about me.
I am a reader.
I love drawing and love my teacher,
They support me and make me keep trying.
I like reading books,
They make me think about being in the book.
In the future, I want to have my own adventure,
With me and dolphins,
And other creatures and animals.

Ummayyah Shakil (8)
Regents Park Community Primary School, Small Heath

This Is Me!

This is me!
My name is Inaaya,
I love my family,
And I love spending time with them,
They support me,
They help me,
They love me,
I am so grateful for what I have.
Every night, I think about small children,
Small children who don't have parents,
I start to feel bad,
And make a little rhyme,
The rhyme goes like this...
Save small souls,
This should be our goal,
But now I'm grateful,
And that's how I want to be.

Inaaya Khan (9)
Regents Park Community Primary School, Small Heath

How To Make The Perfect Ayaan

Let me tell you how to cook the dish of the book!
Add a handful of hope,
A crumble of caution,
Mix with a measure of meaning,
Tip in some thought,
With a dollop of sarcasm sauce,
Lush with love.
Drop in fungi, an abundance of activity,
Fill with a handful of haste.
Include a splash of inquisitivity,
Amplify the taste with some wisdom and knowledge
Last of all, put in some thyme.
Stir, stir, stir like stew,
Until you get the perfect Ayaan!

Ayaan Ul Gani (7)
Regents Park Community Primary School, Small Heath

This Is Really Who I Am: Love Yourself

Hi, my name is Maria,
I like to rhyme,
My favourite colour is pink,
And sometimes I lie.

I like to draw,
I like to paint,
But most of all,
I like to play video games.

Whenever there is a rhythm,
It's my time to shine,
But when I'm in the spotlight,
It's my time to hide.

Love yourself,
Believe in yourself,
You are enough,
For anyone else.

Maria Hussain (10)
Regents Park Community Primary School, Small Heath

The Meaning Of Me!

Seema is my name,
Nobody is the same,
My favourite colour is grey,
Maths is my fave,
It's my last year of school,
I'm always charged with fuel.
Unfortunately, I'm the youngest,
But I wish I was the eldest,
I have two older brothers,
But no sisters,
As I'm trying to end it with a rhyme,
I can't because I have to say goodbye,
Bye!

Seema Al-Shamery (10)
Regents Park Community Primary School, Small Heath

Pencil

P aper is ready for me to write on
E rasers are used to rub out pencil writing
N othing is neater than my handwriting
C learly, there is nothing else to write with except a pen and pencil, right?
I f you know what a pencil is, then surely you know what is inside a pencil, right?
L ittle pencil has less charcoal, doesn't it?

Abid Hossain (7)
Regents Park Community Primary School, Small Heath

A New Person Every Day

I'm about as certain as I can be,
That all of us, to some degree,
Have things even we don't see,
I wonder what I'm going to learn about me?
I know I'm not the person that I will be,
Nor the me from the past,
Shaped by the days that followed,
I'm here in the moment, that's all I can be,
And that's all I can say about me.

Reyel Kazi (10)
Regents Park Community Primary School, Small Heath

My Swimming Trip

One day, I went to school,
It was the day we all went into the swimming pool,
So Mr Crawford took us to the pool,
While we were in the pool,
Rude people were acting like fools,
So we all acted cool,
And the rude people got warned,
After our swim, the teacher said we all deserved a fun session,
And we all lived happily ever after.

Zakariya Mahmood (7)
Regents Park Community Primary School, Small Heath

This Is Me

My name is Rahaf,
I like to play with my friends at school,
And I like to be lonely sometimes when I'm bored.
I have three friends who I love to play with,
I love to have fun with my friends,
And I like to play outside most of the time,
I like to learn at school,
I love reading different kinds of books,
For example, Tom Gates.

Rahaf Albarkoly (10)
Regents Park Community Primary School, Small Heath

Myself: Sanjida Islam

S is for Sanjida
A is for amazing
N is for nice
J is for joyful
I is for intelligent
D is for delightful
A is for awesome

I is for incredible
S is for super
L is for loving
A is for appreciative
M is for magnificent.

Sanjida Islam (8)
Regents Park Community Primary School, Small Heath

Hello! It's Me, Anas!

A ctive
C lever
R eading ambassador
O ccasionally like a monkey at home!
S ometimes alone in the playground
T echniques
I magination is good
C areful sometimes

P oetic,
I love octopi!
E ducated and enthusiastic - I love watching Marvel!

Anas Sultan (7)
Regents Park Community Primary School, Small Heath

All About Me

M y favourite thing to do is read
U ltimately, Goku is my favourite show
S tar of the show is Goku, on
T elevision, Goku's friend is Vegeta
A pples are my favourite fruit
P laying in the park never gets old
H ome address, I can't tell you
A wesome, I always have fun.

Mustapha Bigira (8)
Regents Park Community Primary School, Small Heath

What Is 'Me'?

What is 'me'?
Well, there can be only one of me,
I'm magical, magnificent me!
And you're the one and only you.

Enough about that 'me'!

Hi, I'm Maesha,
I like flowers (I mean, there are loads in my room),
I have two sisters,
And my favourite season is...
Summer!

Maesha Rahman (10)
Regents Park Community Primary School, Small Heath

This Is Me!

My name is Aatikah,
My favourite colour is blue,
My preferred subjects are maths and science too.

My name is Aatikah,
I am 10 years old,
I'm in Year Six and I shine like gold.

My name is Aatikah,
I am unique,
There are hundreds of other girls,
But there's only one of me.

Aatikah Begum (10)
Regents Park Community Primary School, Small Heath

This Is Me

This is me,
I have black hair.
This is me,
I wear a school uniform.

This is me,
I wear a scarf.
This is me,
I have black eyes.

This is me,
I do my work.
This is me,
I have friends.

This is me,
I study in school.
This is me,
Me and myself.

Fozya Jemal
Regents Park Community Primary School, Small Heath

Marvellous Me

I've heard everyone wants to know,
About marvellous me!
My name is stunning Siddig,
And we can all agree.

That I am,
Amazing and smart,
Loves sports but
Now let me actually start.

I am the best,
That I will guarantee,
It sums up everything,
About marvellous me!

Siddig Mostafa (11)
Regents Park Community Primary School, Small Heath

All About Me!

Hi, I am a normal girl,
I like to swim, you might catch me in a pool.
I buy lots of clothes,
I might have left my dad bankrupt.
Alright, I might have been bad,
But my dad won't know.
Fake that I break things,
But my brother did it, don't tell!
My brother hates me,
And I hate him.

Inayah Mehran (8)
Regents Park Community Primary School, Small Heath

Animals

U nder the sea and land, there are animals
M any animals are everywhere, some may rule
A nimals can be big and small
Y ou can even take care of one or many
M any can live in the sea like fish
A nd many can rule, the lion is the king
H undreds eat food.

Umaymah Uddin (8)
Regents Park Community Primary School, Small Heath

Me But In A Rude Way

When you smile, I glare,
When you're sad, I don't care!
And when you tell me to eat, I spit on the floor,
When you tell me to sleep, I bang my head
on the door.
When you tell me to shhh, I shout in your ear,
Finally, when you tell me to stop, I spit on you!

Mahad Miah (9)
Regents Park Community Primary School, Small Heath

I Went To The Zoo

I went to the zoo,
I saw a kangaroo,
I saw a lion too,
And I never knew,
Why kangaroos
Always jump like rabbits, ooh!
There was a really long queue,
I saw a lion plushy, ooh!
And I saw a sign that said:
'Welcome to the zoo'.

Hasanah Sadhiq (10)
Regents Park Community Primary School, Small Heath

About Me!

A little bit of kindness in your day
B eing helpful on your way!
O h, being good is great!
U ngrateful people are bad
T est it out, it makes me mad

M ust be kind, I warn you
E very day to be safe.

Samiha Uddin (7)
Regents Park Community Primary School, Small Heath

All About Me

I am Manaal,
And this is me,
Pay attention and you will see.

I'm full of charisma,
Original and strong,
I am confident and that can't be wrong.

A tip from me to you,
Is to remain hopeful,
And see what it will do.

Manaal Shaiban (11)
Regents Park Community Primary School, Small Heath

This Is Me: The Real Me

This is me and this is who I want to be,
I don't want to be who everyone else
wants me to be,
This is me, I am exactly who I want to be,
This is me, the real me,
This is exactly who I want to be,
This is me!

Amina Arshad (8)
Regents Park Community Primary School, Small Heath

To Be Proud

H i, my name is Sumaiyya
E ager to face a challenge
A s kind as an angel
R eally intelligent, want to try something new
T o be proud of myself.

Sumaiyya Hussain (8)
Regents Park Community Primary School, Small Heath

My Name Is Noor-Zainab

My name is Noor-Zainab,
I want a cat,
One that does not scratch,
My favourite flower is a rose,
I want to go to the park with my loving mum,
She is the best.

Noor-Zainab Ali (8)
Regents Park Community Primary School, Small Heath

My Feelings Grow

I love swimming
Q uestions are how I learn
R eading is one of my favourite subjects
A nd my favourite animal is a cheetah.

Iqra Hussain (7)
Regents Park Community Primary School, Small Heath

Muntaha

M y name is Muntaha, I am...
U nique
N atural
T rustworthy
A wesome
H onest
A mazing.

Muntaha Uddin (9)
Regents Park Community Primary School, Small Heath

All About Me

H appy and joyful
A lways helpful
W orking hard
W henever you need me
A lways there.

Hawwa Afzal (7)
Regents Park Community Primary School, Small Heath

My Rap Poem

I like planes and WW2,
But I wouldn't like to be there,
I'm sure you wouldn't too,
When things go *boom!*
My name's Finley,
I have brown hair,
I have bluey green eyes,
And a big smile.
I like books like Harry Potter,
Yeah, the one with a scar,
Who flew in a car.
I like conspiracy books,
Yeah, I have three,
Please don't judge me.
I like video games,
Like Battle Royales and football too,
This is me, I'm Finley!

Finley Abbott (10)
St Peter's Brafferton CEVA Primary School, Helperby

Ruby Is Awesome!

I am Ruby,
I can tell you something,
I'm the best at being myself,
I have blue eyes and blonde hair,
I try my best at everything,
Like this poem and lots of other things,
Like maths, English, science,
Reading, writing and homework,
There's so much more that I can tell you about me,
I am funny, crazy, imaginative,
And really good at dancing,
And I like to have fun, of course.

Ruby Gaunt (9)
St Peter's Brafferton CEVA Primary School, Helperby

Me And My Fish

I have messy hair,
It goes everywhere,
I don't really care,
I have blue eyes,
That match the skies,
I also like pies,
But I hate wearing ties,
I also never tell lies,
I like fish,
But not in a dish,
They're in my head,
I hope they're not dead,
I have not fed them in a while,
They're probably lying in a pile,
That won't make me smile!

Zander van Leijen (10)
St Peter's Brafferton CEVA Primary School, Helperby

Hot-Air Balloon!

I like plants,
But not with ants.
I like tropical pinks,
Green and gold.
I have a dog,
He isn't old.
I have brown hair and brown eyes,
I like sweet cherry pies.
My life is like a hot-air balloon,
You can make it go up and down,
But you can't control the winds.
This is the end,
Goodbye, my friend.

Emily Dwyer (10)
St Peter's Brafferton CEVA Primary School, Helperby

This Is Me!

I'm a panda lover,
A teddy bear hugger,
I'm an amazing swimmer,
I'm a creative artist,
I'm a book reader,
I like winter, snow and hot cocoa,
I like summer sunshine,
I'm a funny person,
I'm kind and caring,
I'm a little bit daring,
I like school and learning!

This is me!

Olivia Sherwood (11)
St Peter's Brafferton CEVA Primary School, Helperby

Mighty Henry

Hello,
This is a poem,
And it's all about me,
I like rugby,
Sometimes I get muddy,
And bloody,
But sometimes I get angry,
And mighty,
Especially fighty,
I like food,
Pizza improves my mood,
If I'm still angry,
Give me more food,
I'm mighty because...
I'm mighty Henry.

Henry Hambling (8)
St Peter's Brafferton CEVA Primary School, Helperby

Poppy Is Great

I am kind and caring,
I am really good at sharing,
If you're trying something new,
I will wish you good luck.

I really love school,
Because it's really cool,
Life may be a roller coaster,
But I always get through.

So this is me,
I'm Poppy.

Poppy Gaunt
St Peter's Brafferton CEVA Primary School, Helperby

I Am Josie

My name is Josie,
I like to jump,
I am helpful and kind,
A good role model too,
My life is always the best,
I always know what to do,
My puppy, Spot, is really fun,
She is a Border Collie,
I like cantering at my riding school,
I am going to move to a farm.

Josie Wise (8)
St Peter's Brafferton CEVA Primary School, Helperby

All About Me

A kennings poem

I am a...
Animal lover,
Great swimmer,
Quick runner,
Deep sleeper,
Fast eater,
Smart thinker,
I am me!
Book reader,
Baby sitter,
Good climber,
Horse rider,
Art maker,
This is me!

Mia Norman (10)
St Peter's Brafferton CEVA Primary School, Helperby

Me

Good gamer,
Good at Lego,
Good at drawing,
A bit lazy at times,
My cats, Tom and Kit,
Have just had a duel,
Roses are red, just like red paint,
The sun is blazing like fire in the sky.

Sebastian Medi-Sherwood (8)
St Peter's Brafferton CEVA Primary School, Helperby

Me!

A kennings poem

I'm a...
Good baker,
Avocado lover,
Book reader,
Pet keeper,
Creative painter,
Bed sleeper,
Kindness bringer,
Food eater,
And lastly, a...
TikTok filmer!

Louisa Chadwick (10)
St Peter's Brafferton CEVA Primary School, Helperby

Why I Like Dogs!

I am obsessed with dogs!

A t times when I feel down
D ogs always erase my frown
O bedient, loyal and fun
R eady and waiting for me in the sun
E verything's made better by a fluffy friend!

D on't you all just agree
O ne of these completes the family
G etting a new best friend
S nuggling till the sun descends!

Sophie Harman (9)
The Gateway Primary Academy, Dartford

BFF Riddle

My BFF went to nursery with me,
She's as kind as kind can be,
She talks and laughs, cries and sleeps,
And she always plays with me.

My BFF split up with me,
She had to go to a different school,
I still had heaps of friends,
But I had the blues with me.

Me and my BFF made up,
'Cause she came to my school,
We're still BFFs,
Who is she? Can you guess?

Janna Oyedeji (9)
The Gateway Primary Academy, Dartford

This Is Me

T ime to celebrate me
H appiness is a saying of mine
I am as bold as a bear
S ilver lining is what I see when things don't go my way

I try my hardest every day to get better
S illy sausage is what I can be sometimes

M y name is not Billy, but I am silly
E liza is my name.

This is me!

Eliza Huhulski (9)
The Gateway Primary Academy, Dartford

Seeing My Future

Seeing my future,
Is all about me,
Saving animals,
From falling trees.

Seeing my future,
Is such a relief!
I'll have hope,
Like a tranquil reef.

Seeing my future,
Is knowing what I need,
To own a business,
And to succeed.

Seeing my future,
Is who I will be,
Working with animals,
And just being me!

Fairmah Asare (9)
The Gateway Primary Academy, Dartford

This Is Me

My name is Faith,
Some people call me Faithy,
I am very nice,
But sometimes I can be lazy.

I've got anyone's back,
No matter what,
I can always put a smile on your face,
I'll never become a disgrace!

My name is Faith,
And I look at myself,
In my eyes, I know who I want to be.

Faith Francois (9)
The Gateway Primary Academy, Dartford

This Is My Life

My name is Isla,
My heart is as caring as a koala,
I mean I like koalas,
But I love my family more,
At home, I've got a brother and a mother,
I mean, I'm the best because…
I'm as playful as a panda,
I love my life because…
I have the best family of them all!

Isla Coogan (8)
The Gateway Primary Academy, Dartford

Me!

I take a risk,
And discover different places,
I'm as brave as a lion,
As small as an ant,
I'm creative and imaginative,
I'm different to other people,
Which makes me, me,
I love animals,
And I love nature,
This is me,
And who I'm proud to be.

Scarlett Eve Leachman (10)
The Gateway Primary Academy, Dartford

This Is Me

When I look in the mirror,
What do I see?
This is what I want to be.
This is what I'm proud of,
We are all different,
This is me.
If people put me down,
I soar higher than ever before.
I am who I am,
I can be what I want to be,
I can be me!

Andrew George Gray (10)
The Gateway Primary Academy, Dartford

Awesome Ava

T his will blow your mind, I'm a football-loving kid
H onest and true, crazy and cool, that's just the start, so hang on all of you
I ndependent, do you say? That's right, but not in a football game
S wimming and cooking are what I love, take a look and be my bud.

I hear you say brave and kind, take a look and you will see I'm on the dark side
S ome of the stuff I love: Death Eaters, dragons and drum kits, there are loads more, but I've got to play

M y favourite food is pizza and burgers, don't need to buy them because I'm a cook
E nergetic and athletic should sum it up. Got to go, I have a match.

Ava Hillier (9)
The Thomas Coram CE School, Berkhamsted

Kenneth Vile

K enny is what people call me
E nhao is the name given to me by my Chinese grandparents
N eatness is something I need to work on
N ever have I ever driven steam trains but that is something I want to do
E than, who I met when I was 2, is my BFF
T rains are something I enjoyed with my grampy
H ow much do I love my sister? To the moon and almost back!

V ile is my surname, although I'm not vile!
I like reading, gaming and eating lots of yummy food!
L ater in life, I want to be a software developer
E ventually, I want to travel all around the world!

Kenny Vile (9)
The Thomas Coram CE School, Berkhamsted

Nine, Nearly Ten

N ine is a cool age,
I 'm into art and love being creative
N ature and wildlife in the world is amazing
E ven slimy slugs can be cute

N ine is fab, fun, fantastic, fabulous
E njoying playing with my friends
A cting silly, singing, dancing and laughing
R oller skating, ice skating and swimming
L ots of activities to enjoy together
Y ippee! Family holidays, Disneyland and lots of fireworks, parties. What a year!

T en is coming soon
E xcited for my double-digit birthday
N ine is so last year!

Holly Ormondroyd (9)
The Thomas Coram CE School, Berkhamsted

All About Me

I'm Ava, it rhymes with Quaver.
I love fluffy things, sparkly rings, all things pink,
And learning to ice skate at the rink.
My favourite food is spaghetti,
I sometimes get messy, then I play with my teddies.
We go on long walks with my puppy,
We get super muddy.
We run about on the grass,
To make Biscuit tired at last.
I love my friends,
And wish that playtimes would never end,
Even though the games are just pretend.
I get sad on Wednesdays,
But I'm always happy on Fridays.
What's for dinner?
A takeaway would be a winner.

Ava Lambley-Webb (10)
The Thomas Coram CE School, Berkhamsted

All About Me

In the night sky, you find stars,
In the daylight, you will find clouds,
You find people doing things they like and dislike,
You might find me singing, dancing, running or acting in my bedroom or anywhere,
They're what I like, you could say they're my hobbies,
They are my goals and my dream is to be one of them when I grow up,
To me, they are like shooting stars,
They make people happy,
They make people wish,
They are just amazing,
And that's how much those four hobbies mean to me.

Sophie Carlton (10)
The Thomas Coram CE School, Berkhamsted

In The Dojo

Excitement builds,
Tension rises,
Fists clenched, ready,
Gi hangs off my shoulders as white as a tiger's fang,
Bare feet bounce up from the frigid floor,
I bow but never break eye contact,
Hajime!
I charge at them, enthusiasm cascading through me like a free-flowing waterfall,
Boom! Slap! Thunk!
The flag rises in the air like a plane soaring to the clouds,
I won?
I won!
I stroll home, my insides bubbling with pride,
Domo arigato, karate! I'll be back next week.

Elliot Goodison (10)
The Thomas Coram CE School, Berkhamsted

I'll Tell You Who I Am

I'll tell you who I am, who I really, really am...
My name is Billy Kirk, I was born in 2011,
My grandparents live by the sea, down in Devon,
I love my father, I love my mother,
But I'm not so sure about my very little brother!
I like to laugh, I like to play,
It's normally all together!
I'll tell you who I am, who I really, really am...
Football is my game, even if it's in the rain,
If I feel a bit of pain, I'll get right up again.
This is who I am, who I really, really am.

Billy Kirk (10)
The Thomas Coram CE School, Berkhamsted

Energetic Ella

E nergetic, I love football and dirt bikes
L aughing out loud is my number one thing, I am so funny and kind
L oud and clear, determined and brave, I am an awesome kid
A t the track, I'm fierce and brave, don't think that I stay that way

J olly and kind, a daredevil with a crazy mind
O n the pitch, I want to win. Every so often, I get the win
Y ou all think I am good, but you know I am not that kind. Death Eaters are my favourite and you cannot change my mind.

Ella Hillier (9)
The Thomas Coram CE School, Berkhamsted

All About My Life!

My name is Max and I'm ten years old,
When I ride roller coasters, I act very bold.
Most of the time, I like to do sport,
I play all day until I get caught.
I like playing football most of all,
Though I'm happy with a big bouncy basketball.
Tennis is also a game I like,
On a hot summer's day, I'm off on my bike.
Me and my family do lots together,
We do more when it's the best of weather.
I'm always happy and smile a lot,
I like to play with the friends I've got.

Max Culwick (10)
The Thomas Coram CE School, Berkhamsted

One Legendary Ball!

There I was standing on the boundary,
Practising had got me this far,
The umpire raised his hand,
I sprinted in towards the stumps,
As fast as a cheetah,
With a hop, skip and a jump,
I released the ball,
The ball hung in the air,
The crowd fell silent,
Barely a wind rustled the trees,
Then I heard the unbelievable sound of ball on stumps,
Everybody just stood there paralysed,
The crowd erupted into cheers,
The stadium of Lords was alive,
England had won the Ashes!

James Bedlow (10)
The Thomas Coram CE School, Berkhamsted

I Have A Dream

When I go to bed at night,
I like to snuggle up tight.

I dream of happily playing football
With Thomas Toukel.

I dream of jade-green fields
With rabbits hopping
And baby rabbits bopping.

I dream of walking around
the animal-filled zoo
With cows going, "Moo!"

I dream of having four pet dogs
And four pet cats
Even though they fight
Over the mat.

But the thing I'll do most
Is play day after day with rabbits.

Lucy Bedlow (7)
The Thomas Coram CE School, Berkhamsted

What I Am

My name is Sofia,
I like going to the pizzeria.
I speak Polish, Italian and English,
I like sharing, so I'm not selfish.
When I am in Italy,
I greet my family by saying, "Ciao".
In the UK, I greet cats with a *miaow!*
I call my Polish grandma "Babcia",
And I eat focaccia.
I really wish I could get a flight to Rome,
And go to all my family's homes.
When I am sad, I play with my Basset Hound,
With silky ears that touch the ground.

Sofia Fornelli Gajos (7)
The Thomas Coram CE School, Berkhamsted

I Like Being Me

My name is Heidi, I like fun,
My favourite colour is yellow as bright as the sun.
When I'm older, I want to work with fish,
That is my one wish.
I have a fluffy dog, her name is Pip,
Her favourite thing to do is lick and nip.
I'm loud and funny, that's what my friends say,
I try and make them smile every single day.
Football is my thing, I like to rush around,
But also being still with a book is how I'm often found.
My name is Heidi and I like being me!

Heidi Moffatt (8)
The Thomas Coram CE School, Berkhamsted

Right Wing

R un, run as fast as you can,
I gniting your powers to cross the ball,
G racefully galloping down the wing,
H appiness flowing through me like a rainbow waterfall,
T wisting and turning away from daring defenders,

W ind whistling through my sweaty hair,
I magining scoring an overhead kick against Man Utd,
N o one can win a match without extraordinary teammates,
G oal! What a high note to end on, we've won the cup!

Charlotte Goodison (8)
The Thomas Coram CE School, Berkhamsted

The Big Dream

I love to play football in a team,
To play for England is my dream.
It's great to have lots of fans,
All sitting in the stands.
I play for my school football team,
All of the parents shout and scream.

The 'Maradona' is my favourite skill,
It gives the opposition a chill.
I have the pace of a cheetah sprinting
down the wing,
The goalie leaps up with a spring.
My shot is so powerful, it goes in the top corner,
I am a top performer.

Poppy Warr (10)
The Thomas Coram CE School, Berkhamsted

My Rainforest Riddle

If I wasn't on this planet, avocados wouldn't grow,
When people talk about us, they say we're really slow.
If you put me in a race on land, I'd definitely come last,
But once I'm in the water, I can move really fast.
You may know me from a famous show,
Where I work in an office and laugh at a joke.
I'm not the only species, there are two of me,
I have two toes, and the others have three.
What am I?

Answer: A sloth.

James Pierce (10)
The Thomas Coram CE School, Berkhamsted

This Is Me

I'm a boy who likes to dream,
Of faraway places and things that I've seen.
Someday, I'll command my ship in the Pacific,
Fighting an enemy in a battle that is terrific.
Other days, I'm a karter, a racer, a speeder,
Or lost in a book being an avid reader.
I'm a cheetah, I'm a talker, a video game scorer,
And on Mondays, I'm a cub scout explorer.
Now it is time to go and have tea,
I hope you've enjoyed finding out about me!

Austin Jenkin-Seymour (10)
The Thomas Coram CE School, Berkhamsted

Who I Am!

Every day, every morning,
When the sun comes up,
When my dreams go away,
I think to myself, *Who am I?*
One day, I looked in my mirror,
And saw the truth of who I am,
My reflection says a lot about me,
My eyes are smiling at me,
My lips are shining beautifully,
And I love to be nice to everyone I see!
I learn more about myself every day -
Sometimes it's hard, sometimes it's easy,
But this is who I am.

Oscar Nowaczyk (9)
The Thomas Coram CE School, Berkhamsted

All About Me

I think fine things in my mind,
About me being kind,
I know I am a good friend,
Until the very end.

I'm great at sport,
It makes me feel strong,
So I feel that I could,
Race King Kong.

Dancing makes me happy,
It makes me feel so free,
I'm cool, I'm funny, I'm cheeky,
And full of energy.

I like myself, I feel happy,
This poem is all about me.

Lola Rowe-Waller (7)
The Thomas Coram CE School, Berkhamsted

If I Were A Dog

If I were a dog, I would be a spaniel,
With curly, fluffy fur and an owner called Samuel.
My tail is as fluffy as a party poodle,
My hair is so curly, everyone would call it more than noodles.
I run around and say hello to everyone I meet,
Everyone wants to say hello and they give me a treat.
I am so soft and friendly, you want to take me home,
Everyone loves me so much, I am never alone.

Evie Hardy
The Thomas Coram CE School, Berkhamsted

The Friendship Poem

F riendship is a never-ending hug,
R elying on others when we need help,
I t's important to know we are all different,
E veryone should be included,
N ear to others when they need help,
D oing the right thing,
S acrificing the things for your friends,
H elping your friends every day,
I ndividual ideas,
P eople are different.

Rosa Drath (8)
The Thomas Coram CE School, Berkhamsted

My Destiny

If I had a dream,
I would make it gleam,
I would get a dog,
I would lose it in a fog.

I would win a walk,
I would get to talk,
I would make my clothes all green,
And keep them clean.

I would roast a rat,
I would wear a fancy hat,
For my destiny will be bright,
I would have a family of four,
And I would keep the law,
Because I love my future.

Eliza Lines (7)
The Thomas Coram CE School, Berkhamsted

My Cats Are Sweet And Great

My cats are sweet and great,
They are the best of mates,
They make a funny pair,
Oscar sits on his blue chair,
My cats are sweet and great,
My other cat is Fred,
He sometimes sleeps on my bed,
His fur is orange and white,
Sometimes he gets a fright,
My cats are sweet and great,
Oscar's fluffy and grey,
He always likes to lay,
They are the best of mates.

Grace Howard (9)
The Thomas Coram CE School, Berkhamsted

I Want To Be A Palaeontologist

I like digging,
It's the history you cannot see,
What is under the earth?
It is a mystery to me...

I like inspecting,
Feeling and looking,
At the biggest history
Of the Earth.

I like finding really old bones,
And seeing how they became fossils,
I'm happy and excited to find any bones/fossils,
To put on a show to make everyone smile.

Joseph Kelly (7)
The Thomas Coram CE School, Berkhamsted

This Is Me: Ozzie's Rap

Sporty and free,
I love to climb a tree,
I play in the park,
And I love it after dark.

I love roller skating,
But I ain't no dancing queen,
I go to a roller disco on a Saturday,
And I'm living the dream.

So these are the things I like to do,
This next bit is really true,
I love to spend my time,
With my friends and family of mine.

Ozzie Page (9)
The Thomas Coram CE School, Berkhamsted

Me, Myself And I!

My name is Evie, I'm a little bit cheeky!
I love to dance and can't keep still,
I like the way it makes me feel!
Bouncing on my trampoline,
I could fly up to the roof of my house,
I would look so small like a little mouse!
When I try to be funny,
I smile like a bunny!
I shine as bright as a light!
I'm kind and caring,
And don't mind sharing!

Evie Curtis (10)
The Thomas Coram CE School, Berkhamsted

This Is Freddie!

F is for funny, I like telling jokes
R is for riding waves, I love surfing with my dad
E is for energetic, I skip all lunchtime long
D is for determined, I like getting things correct
D is for drawing, I'm creative with a pencil
I is for impatient, I want everything now!
E is for enjoyment, I love having fun with my friends.

Freddie Bannister (9)
The Thomas Coram CE School, Berkhamsted

This Really Is Me!

H appy
E nergetic
N ice
R unner
Y es, I do love football!

W illing to do things in life
I like watching films
N ot very good at cooking
N ot very good at baking either!
E xtremely hyper
T hough I can be annoying, I can also be a good friend
T he fun... has only just begun!

Henry Winnett (9)
The Thomas Coram CE School, Berkhamsted

The Youngest Of Three

Blonde hair,
Blue eyes,
Two big brothers,
And a cheeky smile,
Infectious laugh,
Sensitive ears,
Sometimes angry,
Sometimes sad,
Mostly happy,
Of that, I'm glad,
A big of fighting,
And disobeying,
Also, a lot of playing,
I give great hugs,
And most of all, I am loved.

This is me, the youngest of three.

Noah Cummins (7)
The Thomas Coram CE School, Berkhamsted

Animals

Animals are great,
So let's celebrate,
The existence of bugs, sheep and frogs,
Pets are great too and I have a dog,
Though you can have hamsters, fish and macaws,
Which disobey gravitational laws,
But animals become extinct,
Which just makes you think,
Which one will be next?
So I say, "Let's save the pandas!"

Thomas Crane (10)
The Thomas Coram CE School, Berkhamsted

Zachary

Z achary, that is me. I am jolly, respectful and full of glee
A s athletic as a stunt plane, as fit as a flea
C ool as a cucumber, as sly as a fox
H appy gamer, I love to play Roblox
A s good as gold, as bright as a shining star
R iding my bike all around, zooming very far
Y ou will never see another like me.

Zach Rae (9)
The Thomas Coram CE School, Berkhamsted

Funniness

Funny people make me laugh,
My feelings burst with happiness,
I cannot hold it in,
I have to let it out, *boom!*
My body explodes with laughter,
You can be funny,
Just find the things you laugh at,
And say them out loud,
And the room will be full of laughter,
I am sure of it,
Maybe you will make yourself laugh.

Ivy Thurley (8)
The Thomas Coram CE School, Berkhamsted

Never Give Up

When I find things tricky,
I try a little more,
When I first tried on my skates,
I ended up on the floor.

Next time, I put my skates on,
I fell a little bit,
But I tried and tried a little more,
Now I've got the hang of it.

Because I did not give up on the first go,
I'm now a pro at the roller disco.

Sky Seaton (7)
The Thomas Coram CE School, Berkhamsted

My Thoughts

T his is me
H elpful, always willing to assist a friend
I stand against poverty and crime
S ports are my favourite hobby

I also like art and growing smart
S tanding still is never seen

M cLaren 720S is my dream car,
E ducated and nice, I am thankful for my school.

Josh George (9)
The Thomas Coram CE School, Berkhamsted

Friends

F orever friends
R eal friends
I n my heart
E ven though I moved away, you are still in my heart
N o one can take you away
D ream of you

J oni
O ne + one = me and you
N ear or far, you're still with me
I t feels like the rainbow will never end.

Mabel Thomas (7)
The Thomas Coram CE School, Berkhamsted

If I...

If I could fly, I would go to the moon
And make friends with the aliens.

If I could time travel,
I would go and see the dinosaurs.

If I had a super-strength,
I would move my house to the beach
So I can swim in the sea.

If I could run as fast as a cheetah,
I would travel the world in eighty days.

Alex Newman (8)
The Thomas Coram CE School, Berkhamsted

How To Make Me

W onder at seeing a rainbow,
I ce cream with sprinkles of fabulous fudge,
L ove like the feeling of winning,
F un on a delicious swing made of marshmallows,
R ush like sugary, jammy doughnuts,
E xcitement, exercise, energy,
D epth of your heart, the part that loves you the most!

Wilfred Foxwell-Moss (7)
The Thomas Coram CE School, Berkhamsted

Animals And Me

I am as brave as a bear, *grrrr!*
I am friendly and fun like a dolphin,
I am smart and strong like an elephant,
I am as creative and cheeky as a chimpanzee swinging through the trees,
I am funny like a dancing flamingo,
I am kind like a cuddly kitten,
I am sleepy like my tortoise, Nellie. *Shhh!*

Effie Weedon-Grant (7)
The Thomas Coram CE School, Berkhamsted

This Is Definitely Me!

J oyous and jolly
A lways cheerful
R adiates joy
V ery cuddly
I love dodgeball
S wimming is my favourite

M arvellous at reading
A ll about the jokes
D esiring a dog
O bsessed with Greek mythology
C ooks many things.

Jarvis Madoc Poulton (9)
The Thomas Coram CE School, Berkhamsted

Chester's Life

Hi, I'm Chester and I'm a boy,
I will always play with a toy,
I love my dog, I love his paws,
But my cat scratches him with her claws,
Lego and football I like to play,
I could play Minecraft every day,
I love being outdoors and jumping in puddles,
But most of all, I love my mum's cuddles.

Chester Dawson (7)
The Thomas Coram CE School, Berkhamsted

How To Make Gregory

A sprinkle of football,
A dash of karate,
A hint of baking,
A smidgen of swimming,
A dollop of fairness,
A spot of temper,
Two annoying brothers,
A heap of emotion,
Loads of fidgeting,
A very sweet tooth,
And plenty of gaming, Rubik's cubing and yo-yoing,
Mix well and enjoy.

Gregory Cummins (10)
The Thomas Coram CE School, Berkhamsted

Happy Days

H aving fun is important to me
A nd I can play with friends
P ositive and free
P izza, pineapple, painting and pinball
Y oghurt with honey

D elicious and simple
A nd when the sun is out
Y ellow and hot
S uper happy days I love a lot.

Harvey Skerm (8)
The Thomas Coram CE School, Berkhamsted

This Is Me!

I am playful,
I am kind and
I have a very curious mind.

I am gentle,
I am fast and
I like learning about the past.

I like football,
I like rain and
I like flying on an aeroplane.

I have Delilah,
She's my pet,
And I don't like to take her to the vet.

Sam Gold (7)
The Thomas Coram CE School, Berkhamsted

My Life

I love pizza

A lex is my mum
M ovies, I love them

S ammy is my name
U p is a film I really like
P ea is what my mum and dad sometimes call my sister
E lephants are one of the funniest animals and I like them
R ainbows are awesome.

Sammy Branch (9)
The Thomas Coram CE School, Berkhamsted

My Dream

My dream is to
Go to the zoo
And see two
Monkeys wearing a shoe

My dream is to
Find a clue to a candy store
And eat what is there
Till there is no more

My dream is to
Fly in a hot air balloon
And see the animals from above
While I'm closer to the moon.

Nina Teixeira (8)
The Thomas Coram CE School, Berkhamsted

Me!

T his is me
H umility is needed
I ntelligence too
S hooting stars of creativity

I nspirational thoughts that make my dreams
S hine through

M e, I'm never perfect but always smiling through
E xactly like I want to!

Eleanor Badham (9)
The Thomas Coram CE School, Berkhamsted

My Life

Long, blonde, curly hair,
That blows in the fresh air,
Bright blue eyes,
That glimmer in the night sky,
With a beautiful, singing voice,
I have the choice of being a singer,
Because I am a winner,
I like to dance near plants,
And one day, I would like to go to France.

Kenzi Bonnell (8)
The Thomas Coram CE School, Berkhamsted

Feelings

Sometimes I feel nervous,
Sometimes I feel sad,
Sometimes I feel happy,
Sometimes I feel glad,
Emotions are like stars,
They come and then they go,
Nothing lasts forever,
The moon begins to shine,
We all belong together,
What's yours will be mine.

Winston Collett (8)
The Thomas Coram CE School, Berkhamsted

Charlotte's World

C aring and kind
H eroic and brave
A lways there when you need me
R acing high in the sky, finding dreams
L aughing
O utgoing as I can be
T ired like a sloth
T ough like a lion
E nhancing joy.

Charlotte Nelson (10)
The Thomas Coram CE School, Berkhamsted

Emily's Life

My name is Emily,
I am very lazy,
And I like to eat sweeties,
I want to be a police officer when I am older,
And I love food,
I like to walk my dog,
He is a pretty cool dude.
All my friends are cool,
My stepsister's dragon is small.

Martin-Cooley (10)
The Thomas Coram CE School, Berkhamsted

This Is Me

T aking care of my family
H aving fun
I ncredible kindness
S haring with everyone

I nspirational advice
S plitting things fairly

M aking new friends
E ncouraging others.

Isabella Keane (8)
The Thomas Coram CE School, Berkhamsted

Dexter's Nonsense Poem

D inosaurs do not
E at
X ylophones at all
T o
E xplode tall and short
R unners that have

P igs with
O ctopuses in their
E ars on
M ount Everest.

Dexter Barfoot (8)
The Thomas Coram CE School, Berkhamsted

A Friendship Recipe

Two scoops of kindness,
One litre of sharing,
Three sprinkles of consideration,
60g of helpfulness,
A splash of love,
Two tablespoons of laughter,
A handful of loyalty.

Mix together and you have a happy friendship.

Luke Jenkins (10)
The Thomas Coram CE School, Berkhamsted

Avaley

A valey is kind and happy
V ery friendly
A valey likes gymnastics and swimming
L oves her family
E njoys being creative and likes climbing
Y ellow makes her happy and it is her favourite colour.

Avaley Marley (8)
The Thomas Coram CE School, Berkhamsted

Be You

A bility to care for others,
M otivation for when it gets tricky,
E ncouragement for friends,
L ove to run, it's very helpful,
I mmaculate, clean and tidy,
A thletic is something I love.

Amelia Rae (7)
The Thomas Coram CE School, Berkhamsted

All About Me

I'm very energetic,
Sometimes a bit silly,
I was born on the hallway floor,
A bit close to the kitchen,
I always try my best,
And try to tell the truth,
My best friend is Ryan,
And we play together lots.

Samuel Edwards (7)
The Thomas Coram CE School, Berkhamsted

Joy Of My Life

Joy washed over me the day I was born,
And happiness greets me every dawn,
Peace is my doctor who helps me when times are tough,
And music is my constant companion I can never get enough!

Barnaby Owen (8)
The Thomas Coram CE School, Berkhamsted

About Me

I'm Tommy and I have a team,
Joe, Lucas and Thomas,
After we have a feast of fish,
We play Fortnite and FIFA,
I watch Harry Potter films,
And play football like Harry Kane.

Tommy Hobley (10)
The Thomas Coram CE School, Berkhamsted

The Ryan John Poem!

R eally funny
Y ou will laugh
A mazing
N ever wants to disappoint

J olly
O h so playful
H appy
N ice chef.

Ryan John (8)
The Thomas Coram CE School, Berkhamsted

This Is Me, Freya

My name is Freya and...
I am as funny as a clown at the circus,
I am as calm as the ocean blue,
I am as kind as a fairy godmother,
I can cartwheel like an Olympic champion too.

Freya Harrison (8)
The Thomas Coram CE School, Berkhamsted

About Me

Big green eyes as wide as diamonds,
Long brown hair as long as the ocean,
Small voice as small as a mouse,
Long legs as long as the world,
I am as chatty as a cheetah.

Hannah Manns (8)
The Thomas Coram CE School, Berkhamsted

Lori

L oveliness is the way to go,
O nly kindness kills darkness,
R eally, happiness is the way to go,
I 'm really playful every day.

Lorelei Stanford (8)
The Thomas Coram CE School, Berkhamsted

This Is Me

I am as fast as a lightning bolt,
I am as gentle as the BFG,
I am as tall as a skyscraper,
I am as kind as a butterfly,
I am the best I can be.

Raffy Chemin-Walker
The Thomas Coram CE School, Berkhamsted

All About Me

F riendly and funny
L ively and living the dream
O f course, she loves
R ainbows and raisins
A nimals and acorns.

Flora Harrison (7)
The Thomas Coram CE School, Berkhamsted

Darcy

D aydreaming at times
A rtistic and active
R eading is amazing!
C aring and kind
Y appy and happy!

Darcy Prince (8)
The Thomas Coram CE School, Berkhamsted

E-Bomb!

E xcited E-Bomb!
L oving Eliza
I rritating at times
Z ipping around
A lot of fun.

Eliza Prince (8)
The Thomas Coram CE School, Berkhamsted

This Is Me

J ust a great boy
A mazing
M ostly good at football
E xcellent at piano
S miley.

James Dowling (7)
The Thomas Coram CE School, Berkhamsted

My Dream

My dream is to be a vet,
Because I care for animals,
Big or small,
Being caring and kind to all.

Emily Ainsworth (8)
The Thomas Coram CE School, Berkhamsted

This Is Me!
A haiku

I am Imogen,
My brain zip zaps all day long,
Daydreaming away.

Imogen Freeman (8)
The Thomas Coram CE School, Berkhamsted

Life Is Happiness
A haiku

Sadness is not me,
It is good to be happy,
Happiness is me!

Will Goodman (8)
The Thomas Coram CE School, Berkhamsted

A Recipe For Me

To create me, you will need:
A book filled room,
The cheesiest pizza ever,
A bed all for me,
A cat or dog (optional),
Electronics,
The coolest house ever,
And finally, a happy family.

Now you need to:
Add 15 books and stir in cheese and dough.
Next, add the coolest house ever and cook me!
Let me cool down!
Once cooled, add electronics.
Add a bed all for me!
Finally, a family, make sure it's happy.

This is me.

Jayden Hislop (9)
Thornton Primary School, Thornton-Cleveleys

This Is Me

A kennings poem

I am a...
Bed lover,
Chocolate eater,
Lazy sleeper,
Meat eater,
Steady sleeper,
Biscuit eater,
Big defender,
Subway eater,
Football lover,
Dog chaser,
Sweet eater,
Brave speaker,
Animal lover,
Console lover,
Italian food eater,
Chilli hater,
Wrap maker,
Snow thrower,

Crisp eater,
Drum beater,
Big thrower,
This is me!

River Garside (11)
Thornton Primary School, Thornton-Cleveleys

Weird Girl

I am a beautiful girl,
Kind and weird, cuddly and sweet.
I love my parents as much as can be.
I love to snack and crackle and dance,
This song is my jam, sweet and sticky.
I am like a canine, fierce, cuddly and brave.
I am a fast writer, a meat-eater, a fast runner,
A good dancer and a rubbish speller.
My dog is as weird as a chicken,
Just like me.

Kitty Woffenden (10)
Thornton Primary School, Thornton-Cleveleys

This Is Me

A kennings poem

I am a...
Dog lover,
Book reader,
Xbox gamer,
Music liker,
Enthusiastic learner,
Eager swimmer,
Football player,
Bed lover,
Frenchie walker,
Gecko breeder,
Frenchie breeder,
Finally, I am also a...
Kind person,
Good sister,
Great cousin,
And a...
Good achiever.
This is me!

Charleigh-Jo Taylor-Stansfield (10)
Thornton Primary School, Thornton-Cleveleys

This Is Me

My hair is as brownish as a bear,
My favourite animal is a fierce wolf,
My hair is as short as a school ruler,
I love crafty art,
I am a lover of cute, white, fluffy bunnies,
I have lots of kind friends,
I am scared of spiders,
I hate football because no one passes the ball to me.

Leah Wilson (9)
Thornton Primary School, Thornton-Cleveleys

This Is Me
A kennings poem

Cat lover,
Black lover,
Shy person,
Brave reminder,
Engineer liker,
Christmas favourite,
Organised homer,
Emotional hider,
Family lover,
Clay maker,
Rap singer,
Tango drinker,
Apple juice mister,
Myself lover,
BFF Rowan,
Archaeologist watcher.

Timur Whiteside (10)
Thornton Primary School, Thornton-Cleveleys

Penguin Girl

Penguins are my favourite animal,
I love them more than a diamond ring,
Next, my favourite author is Hannah Shaw,
My hero is my mum, she does everything for me,
I'm an eco queen, that is me,
My favourite subject is forest school,
My name with no vowels is V.

Evie Jones (10)
Thornton Primary School, Thornton-Cleveleys

This Is Me

A kennings poem

I am a...
Homework hater,
Football lover,
Chocolate eater,
Maths solver,
Deep sleeper,
Rabbit owner,
Environment helper,
Book reader,
Fussy eater,
Mysterious watcher,
Attitude giver,
And finally...
Roblox player.

Courtney Leigh Flackett (11)
Thornton Primary School, Thornton-Cleveleys

I Am A...

A kennings poem

Dodgeball lover,
Roblox player,
Dog lover,
McDonald's lover,
Apple user,
Chicken nugget lover,
Paper aeroplane maker,
School student,
Bunny lover,
Honest person,
Loyal person,
And a good friend,
This is me!

Krystian Jegier (9)
Thornton Primary School, Thornton-Cleveleys

All About Me
A kennings poem

I am a...
Forest walker,
Hill climber,
Book reader,
Maths lover,
Fast runner,
School attender,
Dog carer,
Cat lover,
English writer,
Late sleeper,
Art maker,
Story teller...
This is me!

Ava Taylor (8)
Thornton Primary School, Thornton-Cleveleys

Love Yourself!

I'm a dancing girl,
Who loves to sing.
I have blue eyes,
Like the gorgeous sea.
I love my family and friends,
As much as can be.
Arguments happen,
But they still remain friends with me.

This is me!

Emelia Rae (8)
Thornton Primary School, Thornton-Cleveleys

This Is Me

A kennings poem

I am a...
Snake lover,
Family carer,
Lovely sister,
Neat writer,
Great swimmer,
Awesome learner,
Expert finder,
Excellent reader,
Book lover,
Mischief maker,
And finally...
This is me!

Ruby Hill (7)
Thornton Primary School, Thornton-Cleveleys

My Present Life
A kennings poem

I am a...
Gaming pro,
Meerkat magician,
Future electrician,
Nature lover,
Book consumer,
Loud music boomer,
Sunset observer,
Tissue server,
Technological wizard,
iPad glarer,
DanTDM starer.

Samuel Mays (8)
Thornton Primary School, Thornton-Cleveleys

All About Me
A kennings poem

I am a...
Excellent swimmer,
Fruit eater,
Good helper,
Sister carer,
Book reader,
Maths lover,
Cake baker,
Cat stroker,
Late sleeper,
Designer lover,
Ava lover...
This is me!

Sophie Reidy (7)
Thornton Primary School, Thornton-Cleveleys

I Am A...

A kennings poem

I am a...
Taco lover,
Corn shell cruncher,
Chilli eater,
Piñata beater,
Fajita maker,
Mexican music listener,
Mexican cocktail drinker,
Burrito chewer,
Amigo finder,
This is me!

Mason Twiss (10)
Thornton Primary School, Thornton-Cleveleys

This Is Ellie!
A kennings poem

I am a...
Ridiculous reader,
Super swimmer,
Dog devourer,
Horrific helper,
Deadly debater,
Teacher taunter,
Song singer,
Animal admirer,
Money maniac,
Future freedom fighter.

Ellie Turner (9)
Thornton Primary School, Thornton-Cleveleys

This Is Me

This is me, a cucumber eater,
I am a tomato chomper,
This is me, I hate cake,
I love my baby sister,
But I hate my baby sister crying,
I hate dancing,
I love ham, cucumber and tomato sandwiches.

Callum McCluskey (9)
Thornton Primary School, Thornton-Cleveleys

This Is Me

A kennings poem

I am a...
Dog lover,
Good sister,
Cat carer,
Food lover,
Football player,
Cookie baker,
Cake maker,
Game player,
School lover,
Game creator,
Toy maker,
This is me!

Mae Badenoch (7)
Thornton Primary School, Thornton-Cleveleys

This Is Me!
A kennings poem

I am a...
Maths lover,
Fantastic writer,
Cake maker,
Late sleeper,
Supersonic reader,
Dog carer,
Good helper,
And finally, I am a...
Dog walker.
This is me!

Lewis Chantler (7)
Thornton Primary School, Thornton-Cleveleys

I Am...

A kennings poem

I am a...
Book lover,
Cheese eater,
Light sleeper,
Early riser,
Squirrel lover,
Pasta maker,
History hater,
Art lover,
And finally...
Wasp fleer!

Violet Anderson (10)
Thornton Primary School, Thornton-Cleveleys

All About Me

A kennings poem

I am a...
Dog lover,
Book reader,
Pink hater,
Good netballer,
Promise keeper,
Cat lover,
Fish hater,
Roblox gamer,
And finally...
Messy eater.

Phoebe Moore-Rainford (10)
Thornton Primary School, Thornton-Cleveleys

This Is Me
A kennings poem

I am a...
Cake maker,
Rabbit carer,
Sister lover,
Glasses wearer,
Dog carer,
Early riser,
Game maker,
Cat lover,
And finally...
This is me!

Brooke Bamforth (8)
Thornton Primary School, Thornton-Cleveleys

This Is Me!
A kennings poem

This is me,
Having fun,
I am a Roblox lover,
Snack lover,
I am a Sonic lover,
Story teller,
I am a maths learner,
I am an English lover,
This is me!

Thomas Grant (7)
Thornton Primary School, Thornton-Cleveleys

This Is Me!
A kennings poem

I am...
A lollipop eater,
A dog carer,
A cookie eater,
A school lover,
A good friend,
This is me.

Daniel Grant (7)
Thornton Primary School, Thornton-Cleveleys

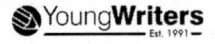

This Is Me
A kennings poem

I am a...
Fortnite player,
Kitten lover,
Ninja runner,
iPad master,
Fox hater,
Bike rider.

Freddie Thompson (7)
Thornton Primary School, Thornton-Cleveleys

YOUNG WRITERS INFORMATION

We hope you have enjoyed reading this book – and that you will continue to in the coming years.

If you're the parent or family member of an enthusiastic poet or story writer, do visit our website **www.youngwriters.co.uk/subscribe** and sign up to receive news, competitions, writing challenges and tips, activities and much, much more! There's lots to keep budding writers motivated!

If you would like to order further copies of this book, or any of our other titles, then please give us a call or order via your online account.

Young Writers
Remus House
Coltsfoot Drive
Peterborough
PE2 9BF
(01733) 890066
info@youngwriters.co.uk

Join in the conversation!
Tips, news, giveaways and much more!

YoungWritersUK   **YoungWritersCW**   **youngwriterscw**